Book 4

All-Star Cheerleaders

Fly, Emma, Fly

Do your best and forget the rest!

For Alyssa

Kane Miller, A Division of EDC Publishing

Text copyright © Anastasia Suen 2012
Illustrations by Hazel Mitchell
Illustrations © Kane Miller 2012

For information contact:
Kane Miller, A Division of EDC Publishing
PO Box 470663
Tulsa, OK 74147-0663
www.kanemiller.com
www.edcpub.com
www.usbornebooksandmore.com

Library of Congress Control Number: 2011943464

Manufactured by Regent Publishing Services, Hong Kong
Printed April 2012 in ShenZhen, Guangdong, China
1 2 3 4 5 6 7 8 9 10

ISBN: 978-1-61067-143-9

Book 4

All-Star Cheerleaders

Fly, Emma, Fly

Written by Anastasia Suen

Illustrated by Hazel Mitchell

Kane Miller

A DIVISION OF EDC PUBLISHING

A Winning Move

Emma looked at the tiny cheerleader ornaments on the Christmas tree. One had her name on it, and one had Abby's name on it. The ornaments were a gift from Grandma.

I love cheerleading, thought Emma. *It's my favorite thing in the whole world. Except for Christmas. And Christmas is almost here.*

Emma was six, and her big sister Abby was eight. They were on the same cheerleading squad, the Glitter squad, at the Big D Elite Gym. Coach Tammy called them the Glitter girls.

These little cheerleaders are wearing uniforms like ours, thought Emma. *But we don't use pompoms.*

Emma and Abby were All-Star cheerleaders. They didn't cheer at games like Grandma did when she was a girl. All-Star cheerleaders entered team competitions and won their own trophies. Their next competition was just a week away.

"Emma, come look at this," said Abby.

Emma walked over to the kitchen table. Abby was looking at something on the laptop computer.

"What are you watching?" asked Emma.

"Cheerleading," replied Abby.

"I can see that," said Emma. She sat down in the chair next to Abby. "But who is it?"

Abby looked at the words under the

video. "It doesn't say who they are. It only says 'My winning All-Star performance.' Wait. I'll start it over so you can see the whole thing."

"We're winning All-Star cheerleaders too," said Emma. She watched as the cheerleaders started their routine.

"That's right, we are," said Abby.

Emma and Abby's mini squad won first place at their last competition. Coach Tammy hung their winning banner on the wall at the Big D Elite Gym. Minis were only six, seven and eight years old, but that didn't mean they couldn't win. They practiced at the gym twice a week for a month before each competition.

"Look at that," said Abby. She pointed at the screen.

The cheerleaders were in a long line across the stage.

"How many girls do they have?" asked

Emma.

Abby quickly counted. "Five flyers with four bases each. Five times four. That's twenty."

Flyers were the ones who went up into the air during the stunts. The girls who held them up were called bases.

"Four bases?" said Emma.

"Yes, four," said Abby. "The big girls have one extra base because they lift the flyers up higher. See?"

Emma watched as the flyers went up into their bases' hands. "Coach Tammy won't let us go that high."

"Minis can't do that," said Abby. "But when we're older we can."

"When we're older," said Emma. "Then we can do all the good moves." She watched as each of the five flyers lifted one leg into the air. Then each girl put her opposite arm up. "What is that move?"

"It's a heel stretch," said Abby.

"It looks like a high V," said Emma. All of the flyers had one arm up in the air. With their leg up too, they made the letter V. "But they have one leg in the air too."

"And they all put their legs up at the same time," said Abby. "It looks so nice."

A few moves later, the music stopped, and the video ended.

"I love that," said Emma. "I wish we could do it."

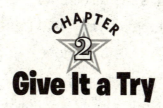

CHAPTER 2
Give It a Try

"Do what?" asked Abby.

"Make a long line like that when we cheer," said Emma.

"But we only have eight girls on our squad," said Abby. "They have twenty."

"I know," said Emma. She looked at the computer. "We won't get to do that move for a long, long time."

Abby stood up and stretched.

"It's no fun to be small," said Emma.

"But that's why you're a flyer," said Abby, "because you're small."

"I love being a flyer," said Emma. "But we don't get to do those moves." She crossed her arms. "It's just not fair."

"Well," said Abby. She looked at the computer screen. Then she looked at Emma. "You can do a heel stretch."

"I can?" said Emma.

"Sure," said Abby. "Do you want me to show you how?"

Emma jumped up and down. "Show me, show me!"

"OK," said Abby. She walked into the living room. "Stand next to me."

Emma walked over and stood next to Abby. "I'm ready."

"Arms out to the side," said Abby. "Make a T."

Emma put her arms straight out. "Like this?"

Abby nodded. "Now lift your leg." Just like that, Abby lifted her left leg into the air next to her ear. She held her foot with her left hand. Then she put her right arm up for a high V.

"How did you do that so fast?" said Emma.

"It's not that hard," said Abby. "Reach down and grab your foot."

"Grab it where?" asked Emma.

"In the middle," said Abby.

Emma reached down and grabbed her foot. But then she started wobbling. *Uh-oh!*

"Now straighten your leg, and lift your foot up," said Abby.

"I'm trying," said Emma. She wobbled again.

"Now put your right arm up," said Abby. "It's a high V with one leg in the air."

I can do a high V, thought Emma, *but not with one leg in the air!*

Emma tried to hold her leg up, but she wobbled even more. *I'm going to fall over!* She reached out and grabbed the back of the couch. "That's harder than it looks."

"You'll get it," said Abby. "You just have to practice."

I can do that, thought Emma. *I love to cheer ...*

CHAPTER 3

Showing Brianna

Emma opened the door of the Big D Elite Gym. She walked in with Abby. It was Tuesday cheerleading practice. The squad was getting ready for their competition on Saturday. Everyone at the gym would be there, even their parents.

Abby went over to talk to her best friend Taylor. Emma looked around the gym. Her best friend Brianna wasn't there yet. Emma and Brianna were both flyers.

Practice hadn't started. The other girls were standing around talking. *Uh-oh! There's Sophia.*

Sophia was pointing her finger at Maddie. *Now what?* thought Emma.

Sophia was eight, but she acted like *she* was the boss, not Coach Tammy. Coach Tammy was kind and gentle, but Sophia was always upset about something. Nothing the other girls did was ever good enough for her.

Emma shook her head. *I hope Sophia doesn't come over here.* Emma turned and looked at the gym door. *Where is Brianna?*

Emma saw a red car drive into the parking lot. The car pulled up in front of the gym door. Then the car door opened. *There she is! Finally!*

Emma ran to the gym door as Brianna walked in. "Brianna, guess what!"

"What?" said Brianna.

"I can do a heel stretch now," said Emma.

"You can?" said Brianna. "Let me see."

"OK," said Emma. She put down her backpack and stood up tall. She put her arms out to the side. *That's the T. Now for the high V.*

Emma held her left foot and lifted it until it was above her head. Then she put her right arm in the air. *High V ... with one leg in the air!*

"Hooray," said Brianna.

Emma started wobbling. She put her foot down on the mat. "I can't hold it very long."

"That's OK," said Brianna. "You can do it, and so can I. Now we can do it together." She put her backpack on the floor next to Emma's.

"Are you ready?" asked Brianna.

"Yes," said Emma. "Let's do it now before Sophia comes over."

The two girls looked over at Sophia. Now she was talking to Liv. Poor Liv didn't look happy about it.

"Good idea!" said Brianna. She started counting. "Five, six, seven, eight."

Emma put her arms out. She grabbed her foot and lifted it. Then she looked over at Brianna. *We're both doing a heel stretch! I love it!*

Uh-oh! Emma started to wobble again. She let go of her foot.

Brianna was still holding her foot high in the air. "Five, six, seven, eight," said Brianna. Then she let go of her foot and put her arms down.

"How can you hold it for so long?" said Emma.

"Practice," said Brianna.

"Oh," said Emma. *If she can do it, I can do it too. I'll just have to keep practicing.*

She looked at the office by the entrance to the gym. Coach Tammy was still inside with Miss Nancy, the owner of the Big D Elite Gym. They were talking about something.

"Wait a minute," said Emma. "We never practiced that move at the gym."

"I know," said Brianna. "My sister Hannah showed me."

"And she's a Star," said Emma. The Stars were the next level up at the Big D Elite Gym.

"The Stars do it in a long line," said Brianna.

"Oh, that's right, they do!" said Emma. "I saw it at the last competition."

"And they won first place too," said Brianna.

"It looks so nice," said Emma.

Brianna waved her hand in the air. "Yes, it's a very pretty move."

"Do you think Coach Tammy would let us do that?" asked Emma.

Brianna shrugged her shoulders. "I don't know."

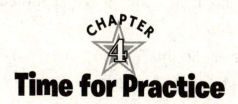

CHAPTER 4
Time for Practice

Emma and Brianna walked over and put their backpacks away. Coach Tammy came out of Miss Nancy's office. She clapped her hands three times. **Clap, clap, clap!** "Let's warm up, Glitter girls."

After the girls did their stretches, Coach Tammy said, "Miss Nancy and I were talking about the Holiday Classic."

"The Holiday Classic," repeated Emma. "What is that?"

"Don't you know anything?" said Sophia.

Emma turned and looked at Sophia. *Who asked you?*

"Now, Sophia," said Coach Tammy. Then she turned and looked at the entire squad. "The Holiday Classic is our next competition. It's a special program before the Christmas holidays."

My two favorite things together, thought Emma, *cheerleading and Christmas. I love it!*

"Do we dress up for Christmas?" asked Brianna.

"You'll wear your regular Big D Elite uniforms," said Coach Tammy. "That way everyone will know who you are. But they will decorate the arena for the holidays."

"That will be so special," said Brianna.

"I know what else could be special," said Emma.

"What is that?" said Coach Tammy.

"Us! We can do a heel stretch," said Emma, "just like the Stars. And we . . ."

"The Stars!" said Sophia. "You can't cheer like a Star."

"Sophia," said Coach Tammy, "be polite and let her finish."

Emma looked at Sophia. *Yes, let me finish.*

"Go on, Emma," said Coach Tammy.

"I saw a YouTube of it," said Emma. "It wasn't the Stars . . ."

"So why did you say they did it?" asked Sophia.

"But they did," said Emma, "at the last competition. They did the heel stretch in a long line."

Brianna nodded her head. "Yes, that's what Hannah and the Stars do. It's so pretty."

"Well," said Sophia. She crossed her arms. Everyone knew not to talk to her when she got upset like that.

Emma looked nervously at Sophia and Coach Tammy. *What will Sophia do now? What will Coach Tammy say?*

Coach Tammy nodded her head slowly. "Yes, it is pretty." She looked at the girls sitting in front of her on the mat. "We could try it. Do all of you know how to do a heel stretch?"

"Hannah taught me," said Brianna.

"I see," said Coach Tammy. She looked at Emma. "And you? This is your idea."

"I know how to do it," said Emma. "Abby taught me."

The other girls all turned to look at Abby. She put her hand on Taylor's shoulder. "I learned how to do it from Taylor."

Taylor smiled.

"I can do it too," said Kayla.

"So can I," said Maddie.

"Me too," said Liv.

Sophia stood up. "Anyone can do that move. It's not that hard."

"Good," said Coach Tammy. "Let's try it."

"But we only have two flyers," said Sophia. "It won't look the same."

"No, it won't," said Coach Tammy. "We'll do it another way."

Emma reached out and grabbed Brianna's hand. *I love it! This is going to be great!*

CHAPTER 5

All Across

"Line up at the end of the mat," said Coach Tammy.

Emma and the other girls ran to the edge of the mat and lined up like Coach Tammy had taught them. Emma stood in her regular spot next to Brianna.

"See how I have you lined up by size?" said Coach Tammy.

Emma turned and looked at the Glitter girls standing behind her. *So that's what we*

do! I never noticed that before.

"Let's make the line so it's taller in the middle," said Coach Tammy. "Brianna, you stay here."

"OK," said Brianna.

"Now Emma, you go to the back of the line," said Coach Tammy.

"OK," said Emma. She walked to the other side of the line.

"Now I want Kayla and Maddie to follow Emma," said Coach Tammy.

Kayla and Maddie walked over and stood in front of Emma.

"I'm taller than you, Maddie," said Kayla. "You stand next to Emma."

"OK, OK," said Maddie. She moved over.

"Liv, you'll be Brianna's base," said Coach Tammy.

Liv ran over and stood next to Brianna.

"Abby, go stand behind your sister," said Coach Tammy. "You can be her base."

"Yay!" said Emma.

"Taylor will be Kayla's base," said Coach Tammy, "and Sofia will be Maddie's base."

"Wait a minute," said Sophia. "This is how we do thigh stands."

"Yes, it is," said Coach Tammy. "That's how we'll do this. We'll do a heel stretch with a thigh stand."

That's not how the Stars do it, thought Emma. *It's not going to look the same.*

"OK, girls," said Coach Tammy. "Walk forward to the center of the mat."

Emma and the girls moved to the middle of the mat. Now they had plenty of room to move.

"Stand side-by-side like we do for the thigh stand," said Coach Tammy.

The girls all moved into position. Emma stood on Abby's left side.

Coach Tammy started counting. "Five, six, seven, eight."

Emma watched as Abby did a thigh stand. Abby put her left foot out to the side. She did a side lunge.

Now I move, thought Emma. She put her right foot on Abby's thigh and stepped up.

Abby put one hand over Emma's shoe. Then Abby put her other arm around Emma's leg. That helped her hold Emma as she went up in the air.

"Put your left leg up now, flyers," said Coach Tammy.

Emma reached down and grabbed her foot. She lifted it up by her ear.

"It's time for a high V," said Coach Tammy. "Put your right arm into the air."

Emma put her

arm up for a high V. Then she looked down the line. *We're all doing it together! I love it!*

CHAPTER 6
More Practice

"I hope we do the heel stretch at practice again today," said Emma. "I love how it looks." She put her backpack next to Brianna's.

"Oh, I'm sure we will," said Brianna. "It's the only way."

"The only way?" repeated Emma.

"You have to do it over and over to learn it," said Brianna.

"Oh," said Emma. "I know that." She

looked around the gym. *But everyone else already knows how to do a heel stretch. I'm the only one who's still learning it.*

Emma took her water bottle out of her backpack. "I've been practicing with Abby at home."

Brianna nodded. "And she's your base too. It's perfect."

Well, thought Emma. *Not yet. I keep wobbling. I hope I don't do that in practice today.*

Clap, clap, clap! Coach Tammy clapped her hands three times. "Let's get started, Glitter. It's time to stretch."

"Here we go," said Brianna.

Yes, here we go, thought Emma. She ran over to her spot on the mat. Coach Tammy started the stretching.

The squad all stretched together. Then they practiced their routine twice.

"I think we're ready," said Emma.

"I hope so," said Brianna.

"The Holiday Classic is in two days," said Coach Tammy.

"But Thanksgiving was last month," said Kayla.

Maddie flapped her elbows and gobbled like a turkey.

Emma laughed. Sometimes Maddie was just too funny.

"Thanksgiving isn't a real holiday," said Sophia.

"Yes, it is," said Kayla. "It's a family holiday."

Emma smiled. *That's the best kind of holiday.*

"This Holiday Classic is in December," said Coach Tammy.

"We decorate the whole house for Christmas," said Emma. "I love it."

"They decorated the stage last year," said Coach Tammy. "They put up big stockings all in a row on the curtain behind the mat."

"In a row?" said Emma. "That's just like our heel lifts."

"Yes," said Coach Tammy, "just like that." She looked at the girls. "Hmm, I wonder if we should add that to our program."

"Stockings?" said Sophia. "How can we do that?"

"We can't carry anything in our hands," said Taylor.

"How will we hold them?" said Abby. "Tucked in our waistbands?"

"But they might fall off when we jump," said Kayla.

"Or do cartwheels," said Liv.

"That's not what I meant," said Coach Tammy.

"Aww," said the girls.

"It would look so nice," said Emma.

"Yes, it would make a nice picture," said Coach Tammy. "I can bring in Christmas stockings for that. We can take pictures before we go on."

"Yay!" The girls all clapped their hands.

I love it, thought Emma. *Christmas*

and cheerleading together. It will be wonderful!

"But what about our routine?" asked Sophia. "How can we make it better? We have to win first place on Saturday."

"Well," said Coach Tammy. "We can do our heel stretch line at the end. No one has seen that before."

"Everyone here knows how to do that, right?" said Sophia. She looked over at Emma.

Emma quickly turned and looked at the other girls.

"I do," said Kayla.

Liv nodded her head.

"Sure," said Taylor.

"No problem," said Abby.

"Piece of cake," said Brianna.

"Easy peasy," said Maddie.

Well, it's not easy peasy for me, thought Emma. *I still wobble. I hope I'm ready by Saturday.*

A Wintry Chill

"We're here," said Mom. She drove the car into the parking lot.

"Look at all the people," said Abby.

"Everyone loves Christmas," said Emma. She opened the car door. A gust of wind blew her ponytail.

"Brr," said Mom. "It's cold today. Let's hurry and get inside."

Emma smiled. *It feels like Christmas!*

Emma, Abby and Mom walked quickly

across the parking lot. They went into the
convention center. A few minutes later they
found the room for the Big D Elite Gym.
Abby opened the door.

"It sure looks like Christmas in there,"
said Mom. "Have fun, girls. I'll see you in a
little while."

Emma and Abby kissed Mom. Then they walked inside the room.

Emma put down her backpack and took off her jacket. Some of the older girls were wearing Santa hats. They were taking pictures of each other.

"Over here, Emma," said Abby. "We have to get our makeup on."

Emma walked over to where Coach Tammy was sitting.

"You'll be next, Emma," said Coach Tammy. She leaned over and put a star on Brianna's face. "Now you're done."

"Thanks, Coach Tammy," said Brianna.

Coach Tammy hugged Brianna. Then she reached over and took a Christmas stocking out of her bag. "This is for our group photo. We'll take it after I finish everyone's makeup."

Brianna turned the stocking over. "Look at all the glitter!"

"That's the name of your squad," said Coach Tammy.

"Glitter," said Emma, and she wiggled her fingers. *We're all shiny and sparkly. Just like Christmas.*

"Have a seat, Emma," said Coach Tammy.

Emma sat down in front of Coach Tammy.

"Close your eyes," said Coach Tammy.

Emma closed her eyes. Coach Tammy put silver-and-gold eye shadow on Emma.

"That's done," said Coach Tammy. "Now pucker up."

Emma opened her eyes. Then she puckered her lips. Coach Tammy put red lipstick on Emma.

"And your star," said Coach Tammy. She put a glittery star on Emma's cheek.

"Now you're ready," said Coach Tammy. "Give me a hug."

Emma hugged Coach Tammy.

Then Coach Tammy reached into her bag. She gave Emma a glittery Christmas stocking too.

"Thank you," said Emma. *I love cheerleading!*

"It's your turn, Abby," said Coach Tammy. "Then we'll take pictures."

Emma stood up and looked around at all of the girls. *Everyone is all shiny and beautiful now. Christmas and cheerleading are the best!*

A few minutes later, Abby was done. She stood up with her glittery Christmas stocking.

Clap, clap, clap! Coach Tammy clapped her hands three times. "Let's take our picture, Glitter," said Coach Tammy. "Bring your stockings and line up against this wall."

Emma ran over and stood next to Brianna. The squad lined up and posed.

"Hold your stockings up," said Coach Tammy.

Emma held her stocking up by her ear and smiled.

"Now look at the camera," said Coach Tammy. *Click!* She pressed the button.

"Let's take one of our new move," said Sophia.

Our new move, thought Emma. *Uh-oh!*

"Good idea," said Coach Tammy. "OK, Glitter, line up for the heel stretch."

Emma went over and stood next to Abby. Abby did a thigh stand and Emma stepped up. *I hope I can hold this!*

"Turn the stockings to face me," said Coach Tammy.

Emma moved her stocking. *Please hurry. I don't know how much longer I can hold this pose.*

PLOP!

"Uh-oh!" said Maddie. "I dropped my

stocking. I hope Santa didn't see that." Then she lowered her voice to a whisper. "I really want to be an elf when I grow up."

"Ha-ha, ha-ha!" Emma started laughing. *That's Maddie!*

The whole squad joined in. "Ha-ha, ha-ha!"

Emma lowered her foot. So did Kayla. The heel stretch line fell apart as the girls on the squad laughed at Maddie's joke. "Ha-ha, ha-ha!"

Maddie stepped down and picked up the glittery stocking.

"Good one, Maddie," said Coach Tammy. "OK, Glitter, let's try again."

Emma climbed up again and lifted her leg in the air. *Take the picture quick, before I start to wobble!*

"Say, 'Glitter'," said Coach Tammy.

"Glitter!" said the squad.

Coach Tammy pressed the button on the camera. Click! "That looks great! I'll make copies for everyone. Now put the stockings back in the bag."

Phew, thought Emma. *I made it.* She stepped down. Then she walked over to put her stocking away.

"I hope you have been practicing your heel stretch, Emma," said Sophia. "You're the only one who can't do it."

"I just did it," said Emma. She looked down at the floor. *I just can't hold it very long.*

Sophia kept talking. "You better do it right. It's the last thing the judges will see."

I know, thought Emma, *that's what worries me.*

Almost

"Follow me," said Coach Tammy. "It's time to go warm up."

Emma held Brianna's hand as the squad walked down the hallway. They chanted, "Big D Elite, can't be beat."

I hope not, thought Emma. She glanced

over at Sophia.

"We're the ones you want to meet," chanted the girls.

Emma walked with the squad into the practice room. There were minis everywhere.

"Look at that pyramid," said Brianna. She pointed at a group of minis on the mat.

"Wow!" said Emma. "I wish we could do that."

"It's not hard," said Brianna. "We could do it if we had a bigger squad."

"But there are only eight of us," said Emma.

"I know," said Brianna.

"If the squad was bigger, we'd have more flyers," said Emma. "Now it's just you and me."

"That's right," said Brianna. "Everyone will look at us." She took a step forward and put her hands up into a high V.

They'll see me wobble too, thought Emma.
That's not good.

"It's our turn to warm up, girls," said
Coach Tammy.

Emma and Brianna walked over to the
edge of the mat. It was their job to lead the
squad.

Emma held Brianna's hand. Together
they walked out onto the mat. Then Emma
let go and walked over to her spot.

Head down. Hands on hips . . .

The music started. "Presenting . . . Big
D Elite," said a deep voice. That was the cue
to start moving.

Emma lifted her head and smiled at
where the judges would be sitting.

Then Emma and Brianna did the back
limber.

Move after move, Emma did the routine
with her squad. One minute passed, then
two. It was time for the last stunt. *Here I go!*

The girls lined up across the mat. Emma stood next to her big sister Abby. Abby went into a lunge. She put her leg out so Emma could stand on it.

Step up. Emma put her right foot on Abby's thigh. Abby put her hand on Emma's shoe. Then she wrapped her arm around Emma's leg to hold her steady.

Now my left leg goes up, and I stretch my heel. Count to eight . . .

One, two, three, four, five, six . . .

I can't hold it any longer! Emma dropped her leg. *Seven, eight.*

The music stopped. The routine was over.

Emma stepped off Abby's thigh.

Sophia came rushing over. "I knew you couldn't do it. You're going to make us lose!"

Now What?

After Sophia left, Abby put her hands on Emma's shoulders. "What happened?"

"My leg got tired," said Emma.

"You almost held it long enough," said Abby. "Can't you hold it just a little bit longer?"

"I'll try," said Emma.

Abby hugged Emma. "I know you can do it."

I hope so, thought Emma. She watched

Abby walk over to talk to her best friend Taylor.

Brianna came over. "What did Sophia say?"

"That I would make us lose," said Emma.

"But why?" said Brianna.

"I didn't hold the stretch for eight counts," said Emma.

"How long did you hold it for?" asked Brianna.

"Six," said Emma.

"Oh," said Brianna.

"I know it has to be longer," said Emma. "But I just can't do it."

"But two more counts are all you need," said Brianna.

"But what if I wobble?" said Emma. "That won't look good."

Brianna shook her head. "No, it won't."

"What am I going to do?" asked Emma. Her eyes filled with tears.

Brianna hugged Emma. "Don't cry. I know you can do it."

"But I can't," said Emma.

"But you did," said Brianna. "I saw you."

Emma stopped crying. "When?"

"I saw you do it at practice," said Brianna. "Everyone did."

"But I can't hold it for eight counts *every* time," said Emma. She started crying again.

"Wait," said Brianna. "I know, what if we

add a move?"

"Add a move?" said Emma. She was so surprised that she stopped crying "Now? Are you crazy?" Emma pointed at the curtain. "We go on in a few minutes."

"I know, I know," said Brianna. "That's enough time."

"What?" said Emma.

The other girls on the squad turned to look at them.

"Shhhh," said Brianna. "Not so loud."

"OK," Emma whispered. "I get it. Wait! No, I don't get it. How can we change the routine now?"

"We can't," said Brianna.

"But you just said . . ." Emma shook her head. "What do you mean?"

The other girls on the squad turned to look at them again.

"Is everything OK?" asked Abby.

"Yeah, sure," said Emma.

She turned and whispered to Brianna. "What are you talking about? Coach Tammy has already gone out to give them our music. We can't change anything now."

"Oh yes, we can," said Brianna.

"We can?" said Emma.

"If you get wobbly after six counts," said Brianna, "we can both do a liberty at the end." She put her knee out in front of her and pointed her toe at the floor. Then she put her hands up into a high V.

"But you can hold it for eight," said Emma. "You don't have to do that."

"We're both at the end of the line," said Brianna. "If we do it together, it will look like that's our move."

"Oh," said Emma. "I get it. But what if I can do it this time? My leg will be up and yours will be down. That won't look right either."

Brianna nodded her head. "That would

look bad too. No, we have to do it just so."

"What if we look at each other halfway through?" said Emma.

"On the count of four," said Brianna.

"Then you can see if my leg is up or down," said Emma.

"That's it," said Brianna. "Let's do it. Whatever you do, I'll match it."

"Thanks," said Emma. She gave Brianna a hug.

"That's what friends are for," said Brianna.

All Lined Up

Emma stood behind the curtain with Brianna. The squad was lined up behind them. It was almost time to go on.

The lady standing next to them looked at her watch. Then she looked at her clipboard. "Big D Elite Glitter," she said, "it's your turn."

Emma looked at Brianna. "Let's go," said Emma.

"We're ready now," said Brianna.

Yes, we are, thought Emma.

Emma and Brianna led the squad through the curtains. They walked across the convention center floor to the middle of the mat. Emma held on to Brianna's hand as they walked to the front of the mat. Then she let go and walked two steps over.

Emma looked up at all of the people in the stands. *Where's Mom?* Emma looked for the Big D Elite signs. *Where is that glittery star?*

There it is! Now I see it. Mom is waving at me. Emma smiled. *I can do this.*

Emma put her hands on her hips. Then she looked down at the mat. *I have to wait for the music.*

"Go Big D," yelled someone in the stands.

Emma smiled. *I love it! The fans are already cheering for us. I just hope I don't disappoint them at the end . . .*

The music started. Then the deep voice said, "Presenting . . . Big D Elite."

It's time! Emma lifted her head and looked at the judges and the crowd. She gave them a big smile. Then she looked

over at Brianna. Emma and Brianna did the back limber together. Then the other girls did their back limbers, row by row.

Cartwheels were next. Emma ran to her place in the circle. Then she did cartwheels out to the edge of the mat.

Time to run and tumble. Emma went to the line at the back corner of the mat. She watched as the other girls took their turns.

And now it's my turn. Emma started a one-handed cartwheel. *Last month, I couldn't do this move. It was hard for me. Now it's so easy.* Emma did three in a row, just like that.

After Emma did her tumbling, it was time for more stunts. Abby did a thigh stand and held Emma up in the air. *I'm flying!*

Then Emma stepped down, and Kayla and Sophia came over. They helped Abby lift Emma. She flew again. Then the girls carried Emma across the mat to Brianna.

Emma reached out and touched Brianna's hand. *Yes! I love to fly.*

Emma let go. The girls on the squad brought both flyers down. It was time for the cheer.

"Big D Elite," said the girls.

The crowd joined them, "Can't be beat."

They're cheering with us, thought Emma. *I love it!*

"We're the ones you want to meet," the squad and the crowd chanted together.

That was fun!

Time for another circle.

Emma ran to the middle of the mat. The girls on the squad made a circle.

Step one, two, three.

Turn, arms out.

Step five, six, seven.

Arms up.

Now our heel stretch line.

Emma ran over to Abby. Abby did a thigh

stand. "Up you go," she said. "You can do this."

I hope so. Emma stepped up. Then she reached down and grabbed her heel. She lifted it in the air.

Emma put her right arm up into a high V. She started counting. *One, two, three, four.*

Emma looked over at Brianna. *My leg is still up.*

Five . . . so far, so good.

Six . . .

Brianna smiled at Emma.

Seven.

Fly, Emma, fly!

Eight.

I did it!

About the Author

Books have always been part of Anastasia Suen's life. Her mother started reading to her when she was a baby and took her to the library every week. She wrote her first picture book when she was eleven and has been writing ever since. She used to be an elementary school teacher, and now she visits classrooms to talk about being an author. She has published over 130 books, writes an Internet blog about children's books and teaches writing to college students. She's never been a cheerleader, but she can yell really loud!

Read them all!

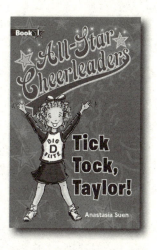

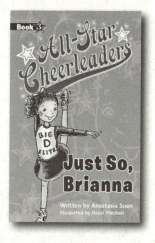